MACHINES MADE SIMPLE

Screws

Written by Kirsty Holmes

KidHaven PUBLISHING

Published in 2026 by
KidHaven Publishing, an Imprint of
Greenhaven Publishing, LLC
2544 Clinton St., Buffalo, NY 14224

Written by: Kirsty Holmes
Edited by: Elise Carraway
Designed by: Amelia Harris

Cataloging-in-Publication Data
Names: Holmes, Kirsty.
Title: Screws / Kirsty Holmes.
Description: Buffalo, NY : KidHaven Publishing, 2026. | Series: Machines made simple | Includes glossary and index.
Identifiers: ISBN 9781534550780 (pbk.) | ISBN 9781534550797 (library bound) | ISBN 9781534550803 (ebook)
Subjects: LCSH: Screws--Juvenile literature. | Simple machines--Juvenile literature. | Torque--Juvenile literature.
Classification: LCC TJ1338.H65 2026 | DDC 621.882--dc23

Manufactured in the United States of America

CPSIA compliance information: Batch #CSKH26
For further information contact Greenhaven Publishing LLC at 1-844-317-7404.

Image Credits

Images courtesy of Shutterstock.com, unless otherwise stated. Cover – Dragon Images, IhorL, Ivaschenko Roman, Mind Pixell, domnitsky. Recurring images – Onica Alexandru Sergiu. 2–3 – Jaromir Chalabala, P24_Design, Heavypong. 4–5 – wavebreakmedia, VectorMine. 6–7 – LadadikArt, Chuchawan. 8–9 – PrimaStockPhoto, Shyripa Alexandr, Serhiy Stakhnyk, rdonar, MikuuuSss. 10–11 – Thomas Hecker, Lazyshape. 12–13 – Refqy, Thaweesak Thipphamon. 14–15 – Petr Smagin, VECTOR2022TR, evkaz. 16–17 – takepicsforfun, Monkey Business Images, Production Perig. 18–19 – Nigel Housden, Jaromir Chalabala. 20–21 – Daniel Schweinert, Edi Umaedi. 22–23 – Katrina Leigh, Steve Collender, xpixel, Flipser, Thammasak Lek, Vinokurov Alexandr, somyot pattana, richir, Nattasid Thapsang.

Contents

WORDS THAT LOOK LIKE **THIS** CAN BE FOUND IN THE GLOSSARY ON PAGE 24.

Marvelous Machinery

When a job is too difficult to do alone, we can use a machine. What do you think of when you think of a machine? Maybe it is something complicated, such as a computer or a car.

CARS ARE COMPLICATED MACHINES WITH LOTS OF MOVING PARTS.

Not all machines are complicated. Some have only a few moving parts, or none at all. We call these simple machines. The six simple machines are:

Simple machines can be put together to make complicated machines.

What Is a Machine?

We need to use forces to get jobs done. A force is a push or a pull that changes the speed or direction of the object it is pushing or pulling. If we want something to move, we need to use forces.

If we cannot make a big enough force ourselves, a machine can help. Simple machines take a force that we put in and change it to make difficult jobs easier.

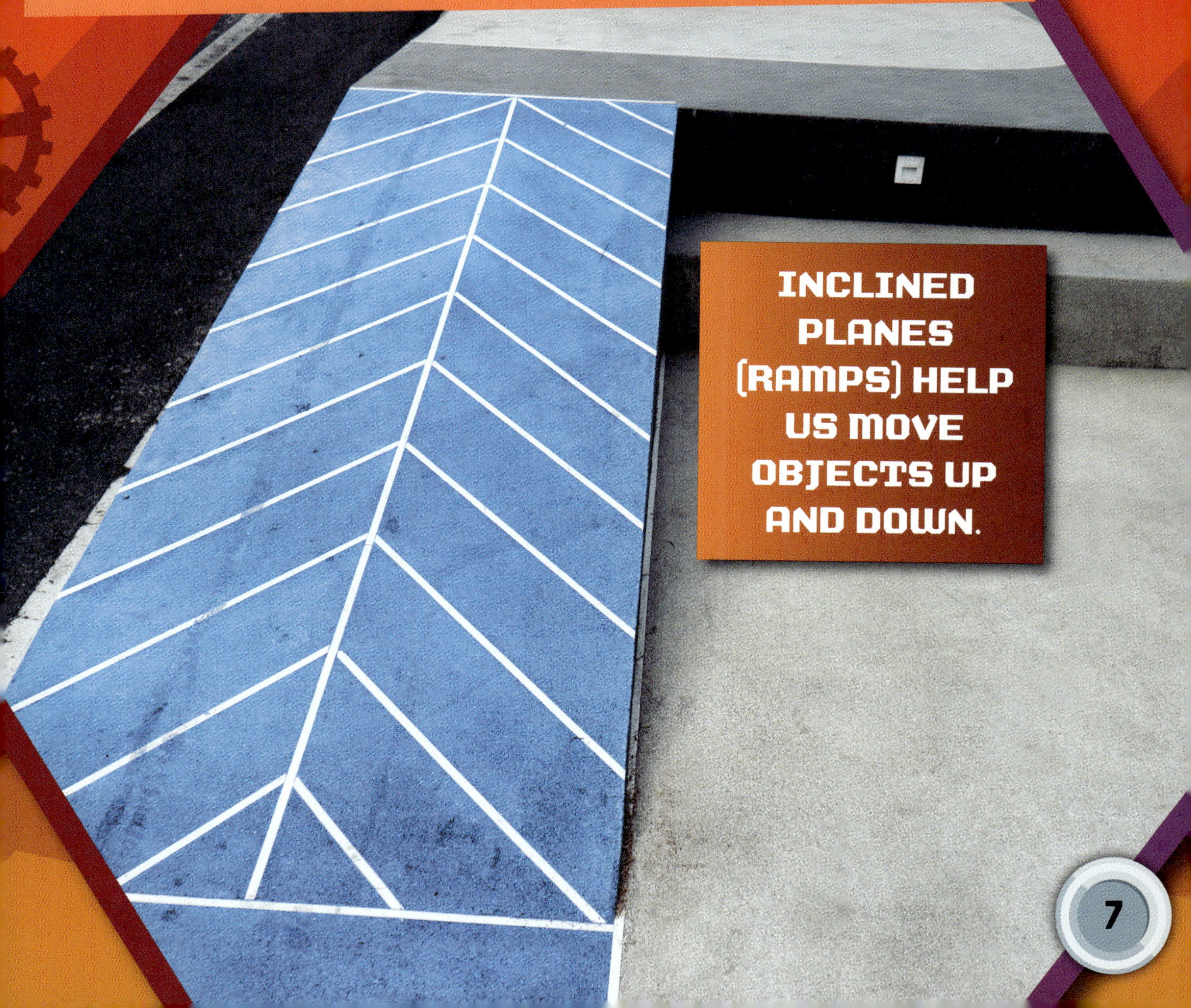

INCLINED PLANES (RAMPS) HELP US MOVE OBJECTS UP AND DOWN.

What Is a Screw?

A screw is a type of simple machine. Screws are used for holding things, drilling holes, and lifting things. Screws do not have any moving parts. Screws are usually made from hard materials, such as metal or wood.

HERE ARE SOME EVERYDAY USES FOR SCREWS—CAN YOU THINK OF ANY MORE?

TUNING PEGS

LIGHT BULB

CORKSCREW

Screws are used for lots of everyday jobs. They can be tiny, such as the screws in a pair of glasses. Huge screws are needed to hold buildings and ships together.

HUGE SCREWS

TINY SCREWS

Parts of a Screw

Screws have four main parts. They are the tip, the shaft, the thread, and the head. The tip of a screw is sharp. The shaft is a cylinder that forms the body of the screw.

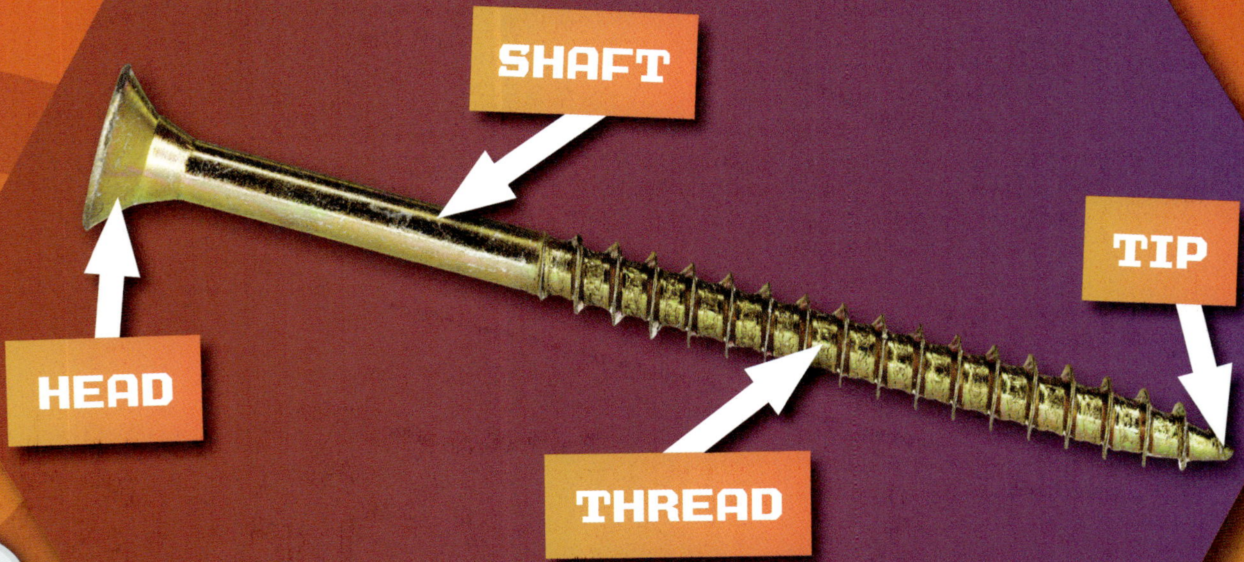

The thread is a thin ridge that wraps in a spiral around the cylinder. This is actually an inclined plane that winds around the shaft. When you twist the screw, the thread drives the screw forward.

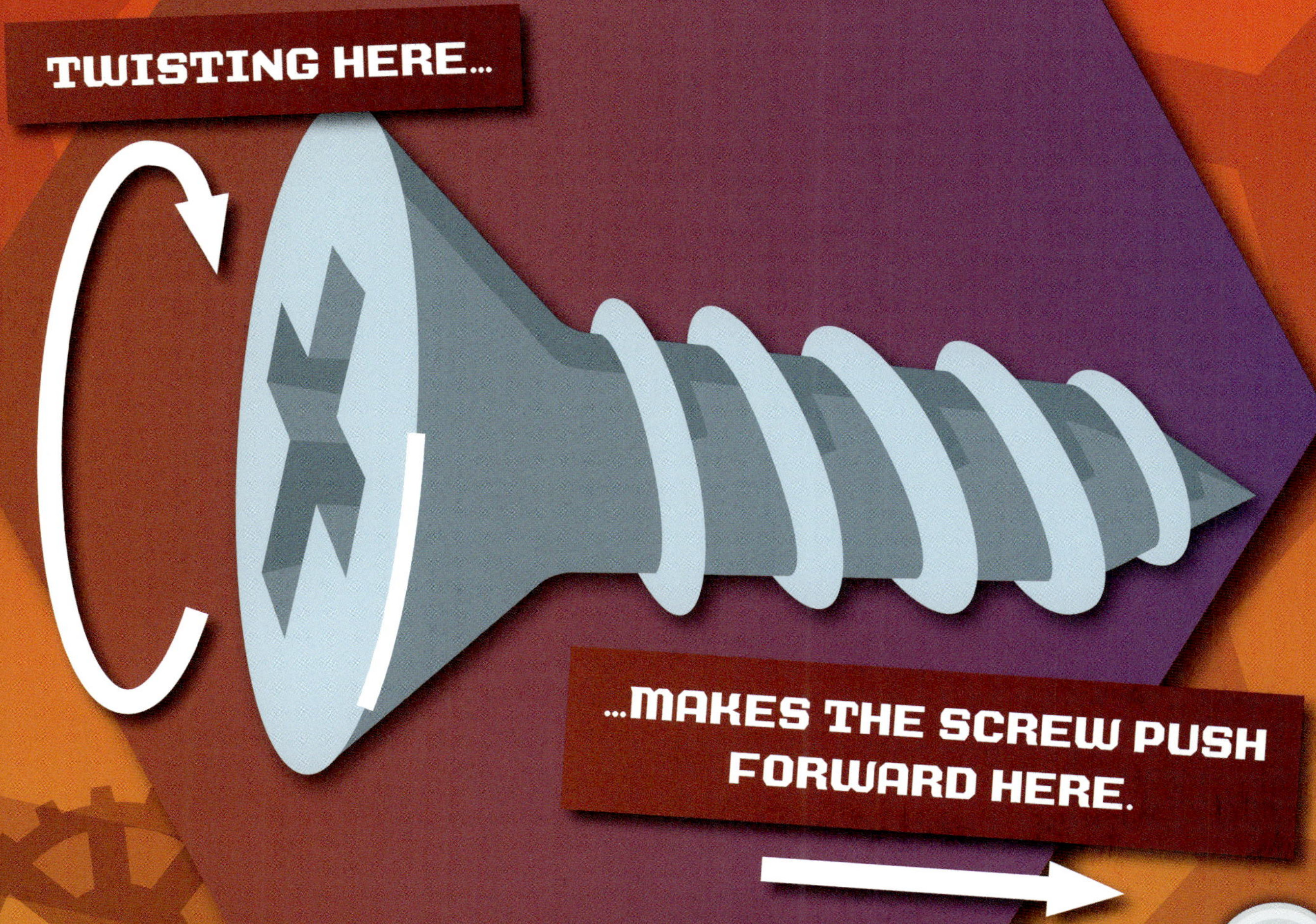

The thread wraps around the cylinder, separated by even gaps. The gap is called the pitch. If the pitch is small, less effort is needed for each turn, but you have to turn it more times.

THESE SCREWS AND **BOLTS** ALL HAVE DIFFERENT PITCHES.

If the pitch is wider, more effort is needed to turn the screw but you do not have to turn it as many times. The wider the pitch is, the farther the screw will move forward with each turn.

THIS TOOL, CALLED A PITCH GAUGE, CAN CHECK THE PITCH.

Working with Screws

One of the main jobs screws do is drive into a material, leaving a hole. Screws that do this have sharp tips so they can pierce the material. These screws are often called drills.

DRILLS SCREW INTO THE SURFACE AND ARE THEN REMOVED, LEAVING A HOLE BEHIND.

Some screws stay in the material. The thread of the screw grips into the material, making it hard to pull the screw out. These screws are used in walls and in wooden furniture.

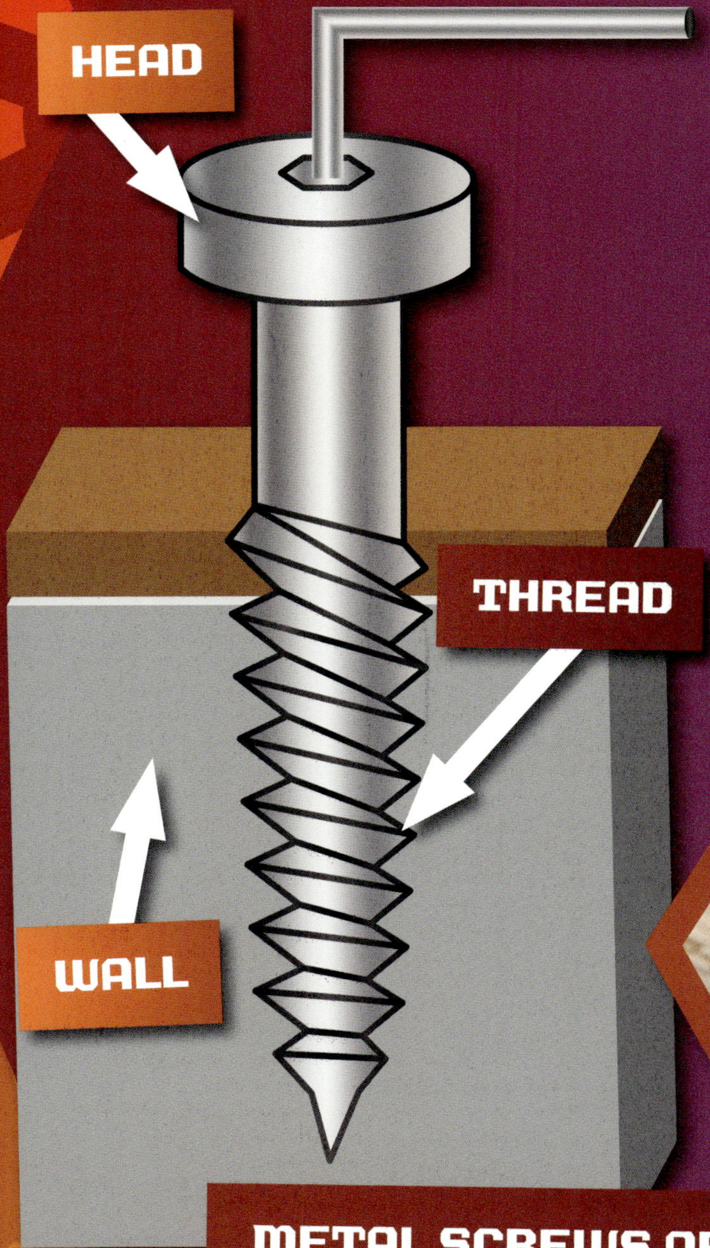

METAL SCREWS ARE STRONG ENOUGH TO PIERCE WOOD EASILY.

Bolts are screws that are used with a nut. A nut screws onto the end of the bolt to hold it in place. Bolts are often blunt at the tip. Bolts usually go through premade holes.

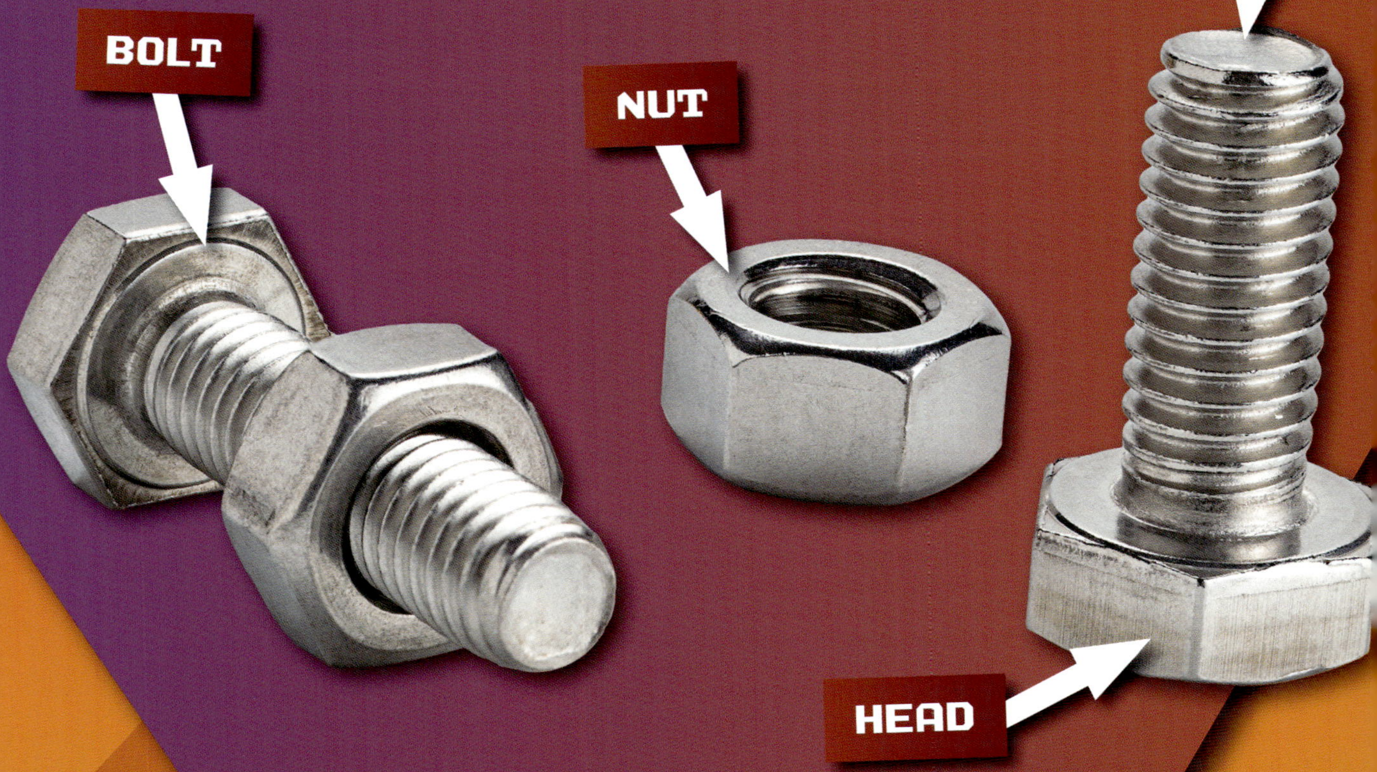

Screws are usually turned using a screwdriver. A small slot in the head allows the screwdriver to grip. The user can apply push forces to turn it. Different shaped screwdrivers fit different screws.

Big Screws

These huge Archimedean screws are used to make electricity. River water flows down the screw, making it turn. As it turns, it creates electricity in a power plant. This type of electricity is renewable.

FISH CAN STILL SWIM ALONG THE THREADS, MAKING THIS A FISH-FRIENDLY WAY TO MAKE POWER!

The bigger the hole you want to dig, the bigger the drill you will need. Huge drills can tunnel through rocky mountains, dig deep mines, or pierce deep into Antarctic ice.

Little Screws

Screws can be tiny too. Computers and other similar machines are held together with tiny screws. Many everyday household items have tiny screws inside. Remember—you will need a tiny screwdriver too!

SCREWS ON A CIRCUIT BOARD

Small screws can even be used in the human body! If you break a bone, sometimes a doctor will use screws to hold it together while it mends. Some people have the screws inside them forever.

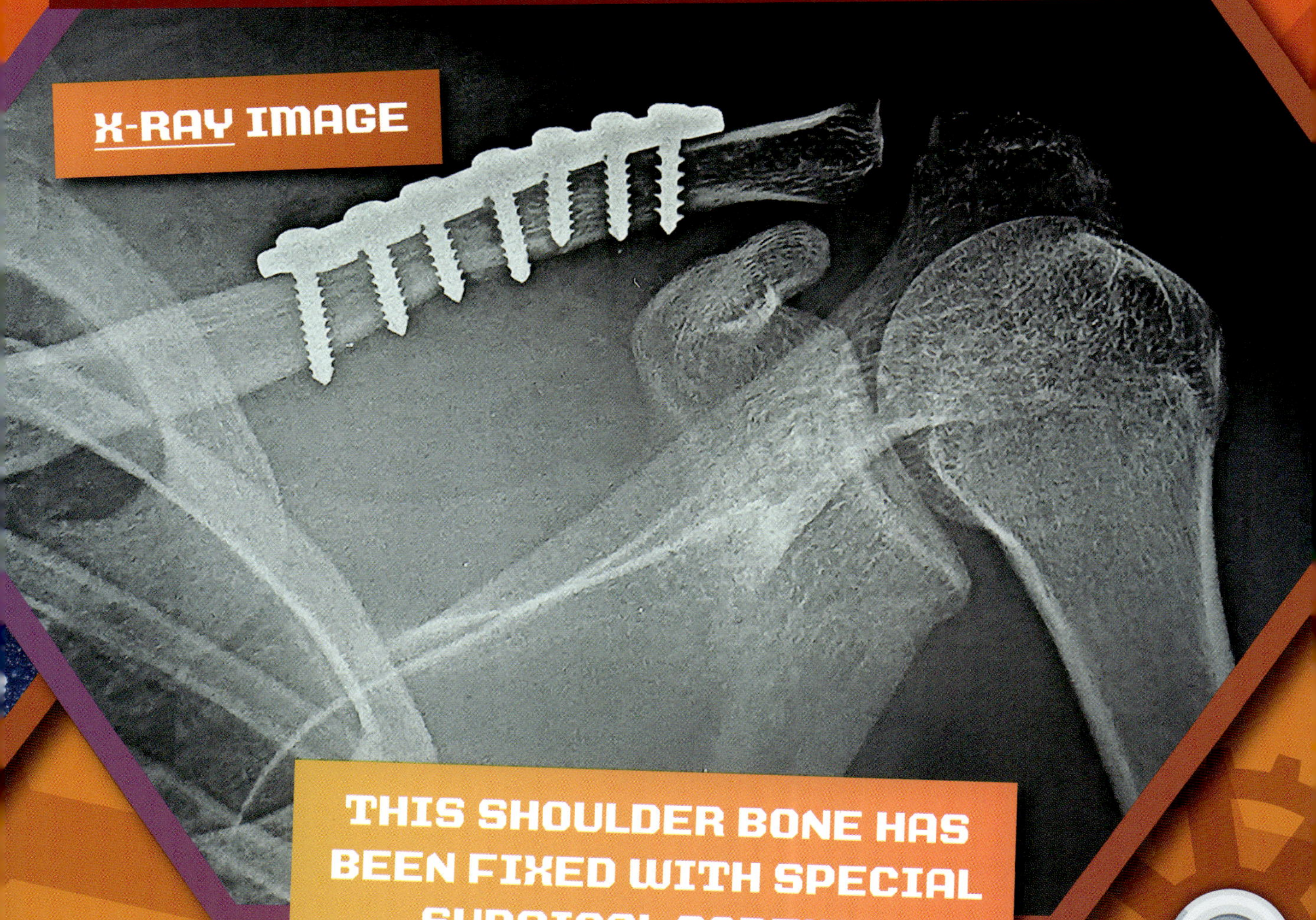

X-RAY IMAGE

THIS SHOULDER BONE HAS BEEN FIXED WITH SPECIAL SURGICAL SCREWS.

Super Simple

To turn a screw or a bolt, you need to match the tool to the shape on the head. Can you match these heads to the right tool?

1

2

3

4

5

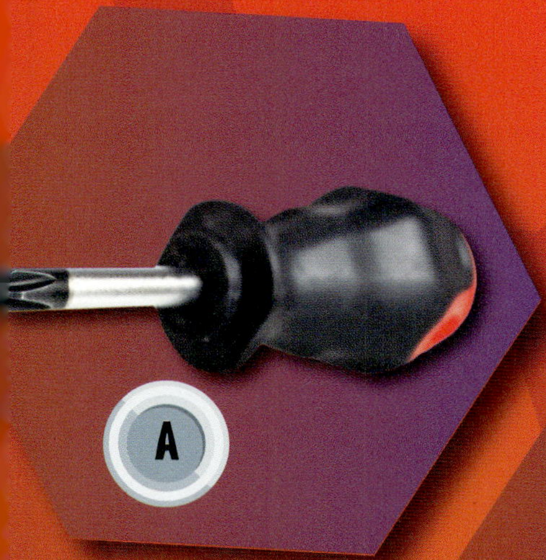

Answers: 1B, 2A, 3D, 4C, 5E

Glossary

blunt having a dull edge; not sharp

bolts screws that do not have a point and are often used to attach things together

cylinder a 3D shape with a top and bottom in the shape of a circle

electricity a kind of energy that is used for light and heat, and to power things

mine large holes in the ground from which coal, gold, silver, and other materials are taken

pierce to use a sharp point to make a hole in something

power plant a facility where electricity is made and used

renewable to do with energy made from sources that do not run out, such as wind or sunshine

surface the part of a thing that is flat, such as a tabletop or a wall

surgical to do with materials that are safe to use in surgery or in the body

X-ray a special beam used to take a photograph of what is inside something, especially bone

Index